John on the Chrysler

John Matherly
1947 — 2004

John on the Chrysler
Poems of Love and Grief

by Laura Vookles

POETS WEAR PRADA • Hoboken, New Jersey

John on the Chrysler

Poets Wear Prada
533 Bloomfield Street, Second Floor
Hoboken, New Jersey 07030
http://pwpbooks.blogspot.com

First North American Publication 2007
First Mass Market Paperback Edition 2015

The title poem, "John on the Chrysler," was first printed by *Ballard Street Poetry Journal* in the Summer 2006 issue, and later re-published by Rogue Scholars Press in *The Rogue Gallery*, an online collective on the press's website. "Unheard I Love You" and "Indifferent Beauty" also appeared online at *The Rogue Gallery*, prior to their publication here.

ISBN-13: 978-0615988306
ISBN-10: 061598830X

Printed in the U.S.A.

Front Cover Photo: John's mother
Frontispiece Photo of John Matherly: Laura Vookles
Back Cover Author Photo: Eric Zork Alan

In *John on the Chrysler*, boundary-defying poet LV has given us a powerful and modern elegy. Tenderly cataloging her late husband's life with clear and thoughtful verse glittering with detail, LV allows us to join her as she attempts to make sense out of what is ultimately senseless — the early death of a husband and father. Heartbreaking yet resilient, mournful yet hopeful, this collection may long for what might have been, but it also shows a profound and brave understanding of what is. It is testament to the power of LV as a writer that one leaves this book — a book so inextricably tied to death — with a grateful sense of awe, wonder and triumph.

CRISTIN O'KEEFE APTOWICZ
Founder of the Urbana Poetry Slam

Laura Vookles is an astonishing poet who rises from life's heartwrenching path only to forge a bridge to all our hearts through brilliant observation and the witness of words.

SU POLO
Host of the Saturn Series

If we consider that each poem is a gesture, and that gesture may be turned inward, toward the poet's self, or directed outward, toward an object or another, this book becomes an opening of hands, an offering not just to John, the direct beloved, but to each of us, reading, a soft unfolding of palms insisting, "I have many train stories, / but this is yours."

MARTY MCCONNELL
Co-founder of the louderARTS Project

Two of the hardest topics to write about are love and loss. So many times they are written about superficially, lacking depth, context, or explanation as to why it should be important to the reader. LV manages to tread this territory with the skill of a seasoned tour guide, covering the important touchstones while pointing out small details that give the larger picture depth. Even at its most emotionally raw points, LV's poetry presents itself with a grace and beauty rarely found when discussing such hefty topics as love and loss. She manages to capture small moments with the exacting eye of a war photographer, leaving us with word pictures both gorgeous and heartbreaking in their honesty. She also writes about some cool cars.

BILL MACMILLAN
Founder of the Worcester Poets' Asylum

Dedicated to the memory of John,
who was my lover, my husband, the father of my son
and the creator of many wonderful museum exhibitions,
including the one described in "John's Railway Season."

LV, 2007

Table of Contents

John on the Chrysler

John on the Chrysler

Smile —
not because he's saying it,
but because you feel it.
High on the Chrysler.
He's just put you there, backed away.
Soon you may be afraid,
but for now you are king.
Taller than your mother's head
as she bends her knees to aim the Kodak.
Your father's stopped by the brick wall,
laughing.
Lazy smoke trails from a Camel in his hand.
He's proud you're not scared.
He doesn't have to say it.
He loves you and at this moment you know.
Later you will wish he said it.

Under a blue October sky,
for a few minutes,
you are the center of their world.
Joy is taking a nap,
your mother and father are happy,
not fighting,
and you haven't had time to think you could slip.
The air is clean and crisp.
Cool breezes scatter paintbox leaves across the drive,
but there is still enough sun
to warm your shoulders through a thin cable sweater.
This is Smithtown, and you are loved.

Later you will forget that sometimes.
This snapshot will be fading in a stack
at the bottom of a dress box in your mother's closet.
You will find it there —
crimped edges soft and fraying —
like you feel when you open the lid to look inside.
The paper trail to adulthood spreads out on the table
as you lift out each memory
until you see it.
Tuck its left and lower edges into your mirror's frame,
and you are smiling out at the world,
loved and knowing it.

Pictures can remind you.
You can't go back, but the past counts, too.
He is leaning on that brick wall —
laughing with his eyes,
Camel dangling from those turned-up lips.
Smoke rises in a halo around a handsome face
as ashes drop on cement,
unnoticed.
He did the best he could.

And you trusted them both
with your feet secure on that license plate —
NY 50 — you are three.
5G57-96 — in '57 you will be 10.
In '96 you will get engaged and have a heart attack.
Now you are dead,
but still sitting on the back of a Chrysler,
head and shoulders silhouetted against the sky,
grinning back love.

John's Railway Season

It was your railway season,
but wood, not iron or steel.
I don't recall what you forged first.
Maybe the wheels — to see if it could be done.
Soaking veneers overnight.
Thonet's bentwood bible, dog-eared.
Cursing when one split.
Cigarette hurled against wet wood.

I rode my first train in third grade.
Straight tracks headed north —
my grandparents took me to Chicago.
All aboard at night by the Mississippi River.
Waking to the wonders of observation cars
with spiral steps and endless sky.

Mysterious massive fragments
growing in the workshop.
People filed downstairs just to peek each morning.
It was your railway season.
One-third scale calculations covering graph paper
discarded on the floor.
Pile of cut dowels dwindling as
you clamped them into wheels that reached my shoulder.

Seventeen years later on that same Chicago train —
this time with my mother.
No raised platforms made that giant smaller.
Towering steel and diesel fumes emerged
from snowy night,
clanking to a stop above us.
We waited, like Zhivago's Lara.
Headlight's eerie glow through falling flakes.

Your strong hands turned pale with sawdust,
coating scabs and yellow dried Gorilla Glue.
It was your railway season.
White's locomotive history,
spine cracked, open on your littered desk.
Paper clips marked paint chips
for the Croton colors.
Only you could see it.

Conductors drew shades quick
so we could not look.
Unflinching locomotive helped a suicide.
Stranding us in dry Italian grassland —
waiting, sick and pensive.
Very dead.
Carabinieri did not come to get her for an hour.
We felt far from civilization.

At work, we picked our way through huge primed shapes,
amazed, bemused, like tourists in the Forum.
It was your railway season.
Our curious waiting weighed you down.
Coming home alone past midnight,
did you dream of coal-heavy shovels,
gaping glowing fireboxes,
shrill steam whistles piercing your night?

I had a pocketknife and held it open.
Jumped down to a dark Arles platform.
Cool French midnight.
Open but deserted station.
Kathy and I waited for the 5AM Lyons special
with three men who thought they might seduce us
if they just talked slower.
I never felt so stupid or so brave.

What spark of genius said that you could do it?
It was your railway season.
Belt sander whine cutting though shop air
so dusty your eyes burned back tears.
In the gallery the exhibit waited —
open space in front of the Gothic depot
modeled after the old Glenwood Station,
built as you took breaks to carry out cut pieces.

Ten years before, a different Glenwood Station.
My train rounded Spuyten Duyvil for a
dazzling first view of the Hudson Palisades.
Nervous interview took hours.
The day I met you,
as you broke for lunch.
Suffocating silk suit in 95 degrees.
You as always — Gap T and jeans.

Half the staff was watching as the pieces went together.
It was your railway season.
Smokestack up on the barrel boiler,
rolled back into the cab.
Cowcatcher on front.
Steps behind to climb and ring the bell.
And us agog at red, green and yellow locomotive splendor.
You, our David Copperfield, and there it stood —
150 years melted away, and no one knew
how your heart broke with tired satisfaction.
I have many train stories,
but this is yours.

Sand in My Sheets

If I ever find sand in my sheets,
I will listen for you smoking in my kitchen.
Lighter click, a cough and then
the scrape of wood on tile as you return to me.
Smiling blue eyes in a sunburned face,
beach mica glinting through chest hair,
damp from afternoon love.

Once more the summer.
I begged you limit work on weekends.
Saturdays in the deli lot by eight,
I dozed to New Age flutes as you
bought coffee, eggs-on-rolls, and Marlboros,
then sped to the Whitestone Bridge
to beat the Jones Beach traffic. At my feet
a bag of towels, Raymond Chandlers,
and the sunscreen you refused to wear.

Before lifeguards set the flags,
we relaxed into all that sand,
sedated by the sun and purring sea.
Reading, sleeping,
then leaning close as you lit up,
shared tales of high school surfing.
You shy Long Island boy.
Flicked ash swept skyward
on white noise wind.

Soaring in arcs, gulls multiplied
with each Igloo unpacked,
and their calls grew shrill.
Eyes still shut, we saw the noon shore
carpeted with bathers, and stirred to leave.
Followed trails of footprints through
heady scents of coconut and picnics.
Dallied at the boardwalk for chicken,
swirled ice cream, and last a stroll.

Languorous in the car,
half-focused on the Yankee game,
we exited past miles of late arrivals.
No need to say
the trip would end up in my bed.
The sun and breeze and freezing waves
stirred senses quite primeval.
You rose to smoke
as sun still slanted through the shades.

If I ever find sand in my sheets,
I will undress and lay my soft back down.
I, the supple hourglass
through which these sly grains slip,
will run my fingers through that warming grit.
My sea-green beach skirt rippling
over sky-blue shag.

Indifferent Beauty

Half-hidden between the desk lamp
and alarm clock, your rose Rookwood vase
has no pride of place now,
not like the pottery on the living room shelves.
But this one I would not risk
to tempt the cat you never wanted.

Just to carry the bud vase in here, by our bed —
smooth, cool and matte with
glowing highlights at the green-tinged rim —
was a sensual act I know you understand.
Five straight sides but no hard angles —
there is no part I can caress
that you were not here first.
Sometimes I think I never saw
a simple thing so lovely.
How did the artist fade that pink to green
without the glazes melting into mud?

I feel the lust that compelled you then to own her.
You looked at me that way — the rose —
the top with tongue-like leaf tips,
embracing tiny flowers,
a hush of curled-back lip.
The sex is no accident.
It was like that for us.

Now I am surrounded by ceramic lovers.
You told me stories of their acquisitions,
but I didn't know I needed to remember,
so they are mute.
But this thin pink angel spins her own tale.
She is Rookwood, the real thing,
and she knew you would possess her,
just as I felt that look close in —
thick wanting air and skin dissolving.

Here in my hand, not high on a shelf,
not just to look at. But too pink, too cool,
fragile, yet unyielding, as life to death.
This perfection conjures opposites —
strong, warm hands, scarred — gentle.
Turning me over and over like that vase —
your very own.
I thought you protected me,
but you were brittle. Not shattered,
but forced to give yourself back — bit by bit.
Even the breath —
taking in less and less,
until you reached the end.
This vase could crack, too, but I guard her,
careless of my devotion.

I should feel more angry at you,
like I am at those Marlboros.
Nicotine that kissed you like a vampire lover.
When young adults ask cashiers for cartons,
I imagine myself shaking strangers' shoulders.
To look in their eyes and say,
"You will die too soon,
and part of someone with you."
Cold, hollow comfort in a gorgeous vase,
and I could raise the cradling hand
and throw, throw, throw
her against the white wall — shrieking —
and all the other Craftsman pots.
Smash, smash, smashed colors
raining down around me.
No tears, just piles of pointed shards —
sharp, like grief.
But you broke first,
and you would be more gone.

Unheard I Love You

I'm washing dishes, thinking about a poem for my son.
I have no ode to Evan and believe I should.
But I don't write that way.
Ideas form themselves and then they push me.
Mists of thought that must be cleared with words.
I have poems for my dead husband, for my boyfriend,
but none about my son, my first love now.
Still, musing, sponge in hand, on sons and poems
evokes persistent memory of his father's last I love you.

Two years ago, bedtime story interrupted, 911 just called.
Thirty seconds to tell a son his father might be dying,
to background stereo of gasping breath
and rhythmic whir of oxygen machine.
Hospice promised help, but now they won't be coming.
Half a minute leaves no time for choosing the best words.
Moments lost explaining he is going to the neighbors.
Nearly six and a half and grasping gravity,
the surprise overnight with his best friend's a diversion.

Unsteady hands on my husband's shoulders,
a reassurance for us both, the ambulance is coming.
First grader's clothes and toothbrush in a grocery bag.
Time for him to go across the hall.
"Kiss your Dad," I say, as he passes the straight back chair.
These things you could not bear to have a picture of.
Over in an instant, then he's headed out the door.
"I love you" floats behind him, low and wispy in the air,
like a ghost already, and he doesn't turn.

I want to cry, "Your Daddy said he loves you,"
but hope John doesn't notice that he was not heard.
How could he bear an unheard last I love you?
Or a mother's tremulous voice pleading listen,
because this heartfelt one will surely be the end?
And in the distance EMT sirens wailing,
a sound that never fails to remind me
of a father's softly sighed "I love you,"
and a poem he and his cherished son now share.

Your Hands

Your hands
were battered and calloused, showed their age.
Told tales of all they had done.
Your hands
were square and strong and stained
with wood varnish, paint, motor oil.
Badges of all you could do.
Your hands
took long boards, sawed, chiseled, sanded, and
caressed them with oil — into tables, frames, desks,
our bed.
Your hands
spurted a perfect arc of blood across your workshop
when you almost severed your thumb on the table saw.
You marveled at the spectacle,
said you probably should have gotten stitches.
Your hands
knew beauty, skimming the glazes and tracing the designs
on vases you collected.
Your hands
painted in wax and drew with oil pastels before I knew you.
I have artworks.
They tell me of your hands — brushing encaustic on paper
in transparent layers, in lush abstraction.
Your hands
were gentle, but full of passion,
their scars welcome on my skin, tracing every curve,
carrying me to places I had never been.
Your hands
washed dishes for me almost every night
because you knew I hate that chore.
Your hands
held our son before I did, played catch with him,
gave him the "super hug."
Your hands
built a wooden locomotive and a sloop inside a museum,

and people were amazed.
Your hands
kept moving, even when your mind was tired,
and your heart was breaking.
Your hands
learned welding to restore a Triumph TR6,
but you never got the chance.
Your hands
fastened buttons on the red-and-black check shirt
that hangs on my closet door.
Rolled up its frayed and faded sleeves,
took it off and draped it on your chair.
Your hands
felt the sting of IV needles again and again,
without flinching.
I stood by your deathbed,
searched your lifeless face, touched your hair,
but realized later that I never saw your hands.
Maybe they spoke to me of life, not death.
Your hands
are hidden in your pockets in my favorite photo of you,
but appear in your last picture, a Polaroid our son took.
Your hands
cradle your chin as you tilt your head,
smiling at him even though you are in pain.
Going through your things I find an old photograph of
a hand
sketching a blue line on a pastel drawing.
This hand
is too young, smooth, pale, perfect.
I am not sure I can recognize it as yours.
I did not know you then and cannot ask you now.
Your hands
showed me many stories,
and I am a different person than I was.
Interesting men have hands worth noticing.
Your hands
were beautiful to me.

You Are a Dream

I have this dream about you,
and in the dream we are talking,
and I am telling you how I know
you still have a presence — spirit or not.

In the dream I am saying how
I've filmed or photographed something —
me with one or two other people —
and sensed you there, too.
And when I play back the video
or flip through the photos
(the details elude me),
you are visible.

There you are
with that wispy gray hair
you wore long for a while,
until too many people said
you resembled Ben Franklin.
Then, when I am speaking to you,
your hair is short, like when
we called you Clint Eastwood.

But I am telling you about
videos, photos — tangible documents —
and how I actually see you —
truth in perception — spirit or not.
In the dream I am earnest, excited,
believing that we can prove
you are still here —
not a light extinguished.
Even a candle snuffed leaves smoke
and a lingering scent.
And I tell you because I need you
to know this, as if you wouldn't.

Truly, I don't understand
what any of this means.
It's all just a dream:
the part where you appear,
a camera's image — just a dream;
the part where I am telling you —
so close — not touching —
just a dream.

Perhaps you, now, are merely a dream,
but I want to think
that I filmed you and looked —
and you are still here.

John's Karmann Ghia

Who knows what became of John's
sun-yellow Karmann Ghia?
Perhaps, as I imagined many times,
a gust of wind lifted the body,
joints weak from rust,
off that chassis and bore it heavenward?
Perhaps it did not truly exist
after it ceased to be his baby —
and, languishing, in another driveway,
the sun simply slipped past the horizon?

But that German coupe is never far from me
when I think of him. One and the same.
Vintage cool and showing its age.
James Dean of the museum staff parking lot.
I hate yellow cars but I made an exception.
Real chrome, with dents and scratches
to match a chiseled nose and
wayward bronze whiskers in a silver beard.
Smoky leather interior like his old bomber jacket.
Engine turning over like a biplane, more bark than bite.

Not a comfortable ride
but intriguing and exciting.
A car to put sex on the brain but no place to do it.
All pent up and screaming for attention,
while John pretended to keep a low profile,
Joy Division blaring in the wood workshop.
Unique like him, a relic in 1990.
I only ever saw one other on the road.
Robin's egg or was it wide blue sky? —
looking for a yellow sun.

Stick Shift Cool

I drive a blue-and-white Mini Cooper
I bought for my husband.
John probably wanted the supercharged 6-speed,
like we test-drove at Lime Rock.
I peeled out on the extrawides,
and we got lost on Connecticut back roads,
half on purpose.
When they were first announced,
he read me monthly updates
in *European Car* and *Classic Motorsports*.
He had a '71 Triumph and a Rabbit convertible
and did not need another car,
but thought I could use some cool,
found my Tercel artistically lacking.
I say that mint-green 4-speed was trusty,
clutch failing and gears slipping
only as my own heart broke down, too.

One day I turned into Mini just to check
if they sold pre-owned.
Only that blue, my favorite color.
5 speeds with surround sound, heated seats
and drive-on flats.
When I sped down the Saw Mill at 70,
I prayed he could see me.
His Led Zeppelin "Whole Lotta Love"
blasting out the windows,
seeing just how high six speakers can go.
Hugging corners, down to fourth, up again to fifth.
There is nothing so macho as driving a stick shift.
Pounding the wheel, head tossed back, yelling —
"Look at me, John! I got this car for you!"
I think I heard him laugh.
The Triumph could do 90.

(Are you listening, John? I wrote these poems for you.)

About the Author

Laura Vookles (a.k.a. LV) is Chief Curator of Collections at the Hudson River Museum in Yonkers, New York, where she has worked for over twenty years. Her most recent scholarly essay is featured in *The Panoramic River: the Hudson and the Thames* published by the Hudson River Museum. Her poetry has appeared in *Ballard Street Poetry Journal*, *The November 3rd Club*, *The Rogue Gallery* of Rogue Scholars Press, as well as in two anthologies, *Look! Up in the Sky! An Anthology of Comic Book Poetry* (Sacred Fools Press) and *HIS RIB: Stories, Poems & Essays by HER* (Penmanship Books).

LV writes memoir about growing up in Memphis, Tennessee; her grandmothers; motherhood; her husband's death; and middle age romance. She has featured for the Boston Poetry Slam (Cantab), the Worcester Poets' Asylum, GotPoetry Live, the louderARTS UPPERCASE series, The Back Fence, Brownstone Poets, among other venues. She won the first-ever White Plains Library Slam, and competed as a member of the White Plains team at the National Poetry Slam in 2007, 2011 and 2012.

A two-time Pushcart Prize nominee in 2007, LV appeared on the Borders website reading "Sand in My Sheets" in 2009. Her video-poem was chosen by Billy Collins among the top finalists from the more than 5,000 submissions to the Borders Open-Door Poetry contest that year.

Since the publication of her debut collection, *John on the Chrysler*, LV has authored two self-published chapbooks, *Love Letters to My Mostly Ordinary Life* (2008) and *LV Counting* (2012).

A NOTE ON THE TYPE

With a few key exceptions, all the text in this volume is set in Monotype Garamond, produced by Fritz Max Steltzer at Monotype Corporation. The Old Style serif font is named after the punch-cutter Claude Garamont (c. 1480 — 1561) but more closely follows the roman letter forms of a later punch-cutter named Jean Jannon and the italic forms cut by Robert Granjon. Garamond is considered to be among the most legible typefaces for the printed page.

Title pages are set in Monotype Corsiva, by Patricia Saunders at Monotye Corporation, based upon 15th- and 16th-century calligraphic designs from Rome and Venice. The dedication, poem titles and other headings are set in Garamond Macron, designed by Paul Kennett and available from the Mäori Law Review site.